1,000 Lives

Tiffany Schultz

BookLeaf
Publishing

India | USA | UK

Made with ❤ on the BookLeaf Publishing Platform
www.bookleafpub.in
www.bookleafpub.com

Dedication

To the process of living.

And to my dearest love, James, whose presence fills my soul with inspiration, joy, and a depth of emotion that words can scarcely capture, you are my muse, my heart, and my everything.

Preface

My heart has traveled.
It has danced through untold spaces, ventured into uncharted territories, and embraced the infinite unknown. There is an overwhelming urge in me, like a restless tide, to run naked in the stars, to chase something more, yet always feel as if I want nothing at all.
These words are my exploration of that duality. I've loved with abandon and this collection isn't just an offering of poetry; it is the story of finding and losing, of seeking refuge in dreams that fade with the dawn. There is a love that lives between these pages, fragile and wild, never quite fully realized but always felt. Each poem is an exploration of that paradox- the tension between desire and fulfillment, between the relentless pursuit of something more and the quiet acceptance of the present moment.

As my heart continues its travels, I invite you to walk alongside me, to explore these moments where love, loss, and the search for belonging collide. I cannot tell you where my heart goes when people are done with it, but I can tell you that it will always keep moving.

Acknowledgements

I find myself filled with gratitude for the experiences that have shaped the verses within these pages. This collection would not have come into being without the profound influence of both pain and love, two forces that have intertwined my soul with the fabric of existence.

To **those who have loved me** - your tenderness, your devotion, and the quiet moments shared are captured in the lines where love blooms, soft and bright. You have shown me the beauty of connection, the strength in vulnerability, and the peace found in unconditional care.

To **those who have hurt me** - your actions, whether deliberate or not, have also left their mark. It is in the brokenness, the rawness, the ache of unspoken words that I have found my voice. Your absence, your silence, has created the space for me to rebuild and redefine what love can be.

For love and pain are universal, and through these words, I hope you feel less alone in your journey.

I followed my heart
and I have lived 1,000 lives
because of it.

1

I have killed a thousand souls in my life
to get to the point of keeping yours alive.

2

Somehow, sunrises don't seem as inviting when you're
still stuck in the night.
And somehow, the sky doesn't feel like it's ever been in
love before.

Many nights, I get so lost in the ghost of you that still
loves me.

3

I should have said it.
I should have told you that the ground moves differently
every time I walk towards you.
I should have said all the things I am hiding,
so that you could have run away from me faster,
and I wouldn't be so frozen
in all of the ways that I loved you.
The ground moved differently.

I should have said it sooner.

4

No one can tell you how or when to let go of a type of
sadness that becomes you.
Falling in love alone isn't as hard as letting go alone.
One is a step, and the other becomes a shove.

With no parachute, I don't care how this one ends.

5

Maybe I am crazy.
Maybe I got so lost in how perfect you felt buried in me
that "too good to be true" just wasn't an option.
Maybe I made you up, and those "I love yous" were
something I told myself instead.
Maybe I was afraid to admit that I lost you,
so I kept you there.

So, maybe I am crazy.
Maybe I imagined a world
where love should be a reason.
Maybe I'll always love you,
and maybe one day I'll know what to do with it.

6

You said the timing was no good, but what is timing
when you could never find a clock that truly
understood?
I loved you.
No clock's hands were ever strong enough to keep
pushing time forward without you.

I wish you'd realize that time doesn't exist in love...
unless you lose it.

In Austin,
coffee tastes different
without seeing your smile
through the steam,
where I unknowingly
sipped both
you and the warmth.

8

In the paralyzing silence,
she stares at the cigarette in her hand,
tasting the years she never wanted,
while he inhales the dreams of someone else.

The River

The boy found his way alongside the river, throwing
rocks for every word he never said to her.
The girl takes walks to that same river often.
She was always so curious about where they kept
coming from.

10

She loved like a sunflower,
and she will always love him like the summer sun.

11

The moonlight lingered on her freckled shoulders,
waiting patiently for his lips to meet them once more, as
the sun had set its mark.

His mistake
is thinking that he can shoot the hopeful out of the sky
and someone would still stay around to love him for it.

13

She liked you -
The way the summer sun gently warmed his face,
laughing the stars out of hiding together every time.
She loved you.

14

"The pain is unbearable." She said to her mom. "The pain is like being dropped from a fifty-foot building and still somehow surviving as nothing."

15

Sinking my teeth into the desired curves on your neck
would be sweeter than biting my tongue
just to taste the blood that isn't yours.

16

Someone will love me the way I loved you, but they won't survive me.
We will kill souls while searching for each other among the passengers traveling through our empty lives.

17

There was always something about the way his hand met the small of my back every time we walked into a room.

He was always so gentle in the ways he wanted to own me.

18

The smell of your home invited me in.
It was every scent, all together,
that had once wrapped itself around me.
Your floor held my tears, my laughter, and my love.

And no matter how much you've swept since then,
that's all I saw beneath your furniture as I stood there,
saying goodbye.

19

I'm diving into an ocean scene where I mean nothing to
it, upon this ledge.
Just like you, I am standing in front of something so vast,
without any power to be noticed,
while the storms brew in the distance.
Your distance.
The angry waves, your angry heart.
I feel so small. I feel so small.
I can't seem to stop looking up toward its destruction,
for the love that I have cannot be moved.

20

She turned into a stained piece of art
from the back of the shelf,
where dust obscured her view
of the room, the world, and him.

21

My dearest love,
You have taken my days,
which were once filled with despair,
and covered them with exuberance.
You came back to me.
You traveled through lives
and called my freckles constellations.
Maybe they are what guided you home.
For every atom that I am made of,
you named each specific one to show me
how alive I can feel while living inside of your love.
I made my way back to you, too.

My dearest love,
They say when life gives you lemons,
you make lemonade.
But life gave me you instead, so I created art,
and it tastes so much sweeter.
I love you. I love you.

www.ingramcontent.com/pod-product-compliance
Lightning Source LLC
La Vergne TN
LVHW051249200726
843510LV00011B/1763